Praise for
Humble Orthodoxy

"I suppose the opposite of humble orthodoxy is arrogant orthodoxy—a rather ugly pairing of words since 'orthodoxy' takes us
to King Jesus, who is 'gentle and humble in heart.' Defending
orthodoxy, a perennially urgent responsibility, so easily degen-
erates into our defending ourselves and our opinions, a perennially deceptive form of idolatry. May this short book by Joshua
Harris encourage many to love and articulate the truth with the
same tears of compassion that Jesus shed over the city."

—D. A. CARSON, research professor of New Testament
at Trinity Evangelical Divinity School, Deerfield, IL,
and author of *The Intolerance of Tolerance*

"When I think of the words 'humble orthodoxy,' I think immediately of Josh Harris. In this book you will find not merely
an expert calling us to an abstract idea. You will find the heart
of a man who demonstrates humility and conviction, mostly
in ways that he doesn't see himself (or he wouldn't be qualified
to write this book). *Humble Orthodoxy* will show you, with
authenticity and vulnerability, what it means to realize that,
left to ourselves, we are all arrogant heretics. But the Spirit of
God can crucify our pride and our unfaithfulness. I heartily
commend this good, practical book."

—RUSSELL D. MOORE, dean, Southern Baptist
Theological Seminary, Louisville, KY, and author
of *Tempted and Tried: Temptation and the Triumph
of Christ*

"When many years ago I first heard my good friend Josh Harris talk about the need for 'humble orthodoxy,' the phrase resonated with me immediately. Because, as Calvin said, the heart is an idol-making factory, we often take a good thing and make it an ultimate thing. We take something that is meant to help people, and we use it in hurtful ways. Sadly, many thinking Christians do this with doctrine. We argue for the glory of God in an unglorious manner. Josh knows this and is on a mission to change the tone of our theological conversations and put doctrine in its rightful place—as a servant to all but a master to none. He understands that if we dot all our doctrinal i's and cross all our doctrinal t's but have not love, we will be nothing more than 'a noisy gong or a clanging cymbal.' Thanks for this, Josh. A much-needed message for our time."

—TULLIAN TCHIVIDJIAN, pastor of Coral Ridge Presbyterian Church, Fort Lauderdale, FL, and author of *Jesus + Nothing = Everything*

"I love the message of *Humble Orthodoxy*. It further fueled the fire within me for a passionate commitment to truth that would put me on my knees instead of puffing me up. God is opposed to the proud but gives grace to the humble. I pray that God will use the message of this book to topple tall towers of pride that are so out of place in the church of Jesus Christ. May pure worship flow from humble orthodoxy!"

—JASON MEYER, pastor of preaching and vision, Bethlehem Baptist Church, Minneapolis, MN

humble

ORTHODOXY

holding the truth high without putting people down

JOSHUA HARRIS

with ERIC STANFORD

FOREWORD BY J. D. GREEAR

MULTNOMAH
BOOKS

HUMBLE ORTHODOXY
PUBLISHED BY MULTNOMAH BOOKS
12265 Oracle Boulevard, Suite 200
Colorado Springs, Colorado 80921

All Scripture quotations, unless otherwise indicated, are taken from The Holy Bible,
English Standard Version, copyright © 2001 by Crossway Bibles, a division of Good
News Publishers. Used by permission. Scripture quotations marked
(NIV) are taken from the Holy Bible, New International Version®, NIV®. Copyright ©
1973, 1978, 1984 by Biblica Inc.™ Used by permission of Zondervan. All rights reserved
worldwide. www.zondervan.com.

Hardcover ISBN: 978-1-60142-475-4
eBook ISBN: 978-1-60142-476-1

Cover design by Kristopher K. Orr; cover image by RF Images

Content in this book is drawn from and is an expansion of the chapter "Humble
Orthodoxy" in *Dug Down Deep*, copyright © 2010 by Joshua Harris, published by
Multnomah Books.

Published in the United States by WaterBrook Multnomah, an imprint of the Crown
Publishing Group, a division of Random House Inc., New York.

MULTNOMAH and its mountain colophon are registered trademarks of Random House Inc.

Library of Congress Cataloging-in-Publication Data
Harris, Joshua.
        Humble orthodoxy : holding the truth high without putting people down / Joshua
Harris, with Eric Stanford. — 1st ed.
          p. cm.
        ISBN 978-1-60142-475-4 — ISBN 978-1-60142-476-1 (electronic)
    1. Christian life. I. Stanford, Eric. II. Title.
        BV4501.3.H375 2013
        248.4—dc23

                                                            2012042305

Printed in the United States of America
2013—First Edition

10 9 8 7 6 5 4 3 2 1

SPECIAL SALES
Most WaterBrook Multnomah books are available at special quantity discounts when
purchased in bulk by corporations, organizations, and special-interest groups. Custom
imprinting or excerpting can also be done to fit special needs. For information, please
e-mail SpecialMarkets@WaterBrookMultnomah.com or call 1-800-603-7051.

To Robin Boisvert,
a faithful friend and pastor

Contents

Foreword

Followers of Jesus *want* to be like our Lord. And maybe we *think* we are. But all too often we're really more like the group Jesus warned about most frequently: the Pharisees. Sadly, the journey into Pharisaism is an easy one.

In Jesus's day the Pharisees were not a bad group. In fact, they were the orthodox group with the right doctrines and the right zeal for the faith of their fathers. They were the guys you wanted to speak at your conference and whose books topped the bestseller lists. Yet not only did they miss the Son of God when he stood before them, but they actually helped crucify him.

The Holy Spirit did not go into such detail about the Pharisees in the New Testament just so we could understand a group unique to the first century. Pharisaism is a poisonous weed that grows in every garden of orthodox religion. Pharisaism is every bit the threat to the orthodox today that it was then.

Pharisaism has less to do with what doctrines we hold than with *how* we hold them. As Josh Harris shows in this book, getting doctrine right is a matter of life and death, but holding that doctrine in the right spirit is essential too. A great deal of damage is done by those who hold the truth of Christ with the spirit of Satan. Knowledge in their hands becomes a tool for puffing up, which produces pride, which leads not to life but to "the condemnation of the devil" (1 Timothy 3:6).

Consequently, I can think of few books as pressing for our moment as this one. In this helpful, accessible work, Josh presents us with gospel truth and does it in the generosity of spirit the gospel produces.

I love Josh Harris both as a writer and as a friend. He radiates love and humility, not only toward Jesus, but also toward the church. His commitment to the Word challenges and inspires me. His love for Jesus and for Jesus's people humbles me.

The truths presented in these pages lead me to worship. And then repent. I believe they will do so for you as well. So I challenge you to study them, not in the way a seminarian studies doctrine, but in the way you might study a sunset that leaves you speechless.

Throughout this book you'll find yourself wanting to set the book down and lift your eyes upward. Or write a letter of apology. Obey those impulses. That is faith working through love, and that is the goal of the gospel.

> —J. D. Greear, senior pastor, The Summit
> Church, Durham, North Carolina; author
> of *Gospel: Recovering the Power that Made
> Christianity Revolutionary*

Follow the pattern of the sound words
that you have heard from me, in the faith
and love that are in Christ Jesus. By the
Holy Spirit who dwells within us, guard
the good deposit entrusted to you.
—2 Timothy 1:13–14

Have nothing to do with foolish, ignorant
controversies; you know that they breed
quarrels. And the Lord's servant must
not be quarrelsome but kind to everyone,
able to teach, patiently enduring evil,
correcting his opponents with gentleness.
God may perhaps grant them repentance
leading to a knowledge of the truth.
—2 Timothy 2:23–25

1

Your Attitude Matters

A few years ago I was in Seattle with an old friend who had written a popular book about his personal reflections and experiences with the Christian faith. He began telling me about the e-mails he was getting from readers. He said the harshest ones were from people who presented themselves as "caring about doctrine." Their e-mails were vitriolic, pointing out the theological errors and inconsistencies of what he had written.

My friend isn't a pastor or a Bible scholar. He's a poet and a storyteller. That's part of what makes his writing appealing. Honestly, he did get some things wrong in his book. I think he knows that. But I saw how hard it was for him to admit that he might have a problem with orthodoxy when the information was coming from people whose words and attitudes were ugly.

The word *orthodoxy* refers to right thinking about God.

It's about teaching and belief based on the established, proven, cherished truths of the faith. These are the truths that don't budge. They are the plumb line that shows us how to think straight in a crooked world. They're clearly taught in Scripture and affirmed in the historic creeds of the Christian faith:

- There is one God who created all things.
- God is triune: Father, Son, and Holy Spirit.
- The Bible is God's inerrant word to humanity.
- Jesus is the virgin-born, eternal Son of God.
- Jesus died as a substitute for sinners so they could be forgiven.
- Jesus rose from the dead.
- Jesus will one day return to judge the world.

Orthodox beliefs have been acknowledged by genuine followers of Jesus from the beginning and handed down through the ages. Take one of them away, and you're left with something less than historic Christian belief.

But one of the problems with the word *orthodoxy* is that it is usually brought up when someone is being reprimanded. So it has gotten a bad reputation, like an older sibling who is always peeking around the corner, trying to catch you doing something wrong.

I think every generation of Christians faces the temptation to buck orthodoxy for just this reason. Even if we know something is true and right, we don't like others telling us we have to believe it. And if our own pride weren't influence enough, the temptation to abandon orthodoxy intensifies when its advocates are unlikable and meanspirited.

> Orthodox truths are the plumb line that shows us how to think straight in a crooked world.

I don't know any other way to say this: it seems like a lot of the people who care about orthodoxy are jerks.

But why? Does good doctrine necessarily lead to being argumentative, annoying, and arrogant?

HUMBLE ORTHODOXY

My friend Eric says that what Christians today need is *humble orthodoxy.* I like that phrase. Christians need to have a strong commitment to sound doctrine. We need to be courageous in our stand for biblical truth. But we also need to be gracious in our words and interaction with other people.

Whether our theological knowledge is great or small, we all need to ask a vital question: What will we do with the knowledge of God that we have?

Will it lead us to an ever-growing desire to know and love the Lord? Will it practically affect the way we think and live? Will we have the courage to hold on to the truth even when it isn't popular? And how will we express our beliefs? With humility—or with pride?

I don't want to be like the people who wrote angry letters to my Seattle friend. At the same time, I don't want to be like some well-intentioned people I know who are careless, almost unconcerned, about Christian truths. They never make others feel uncomfortable about their beliefs, but that's because they believe hardly anything themselves.

Do we have to choose between kindness and a zeal for truth? Does embracing deeply held beliefs require that we let go of humility?

And this brings us to a bigger question: Does any of this matter to God? Does God's Word speak to the priority of both humility and orthodoxy? Or is this all just a matter of personality—some people are nice, some people care about doctrine?

Here's what I believe: truth matters...but so does our attitude. This is what I mean by *humble orthodoxy:* we must care deeply about truth, and we must also defend and share this truth with compassion and humility.

> We must care deeply about truth, and we must also defend and share this truth with compassion and humility.

God has given the saving message of the gospel to his people through his Word, and we must be willing to fight for its integrity and faithful transmission. We are to "contend for the faith that was once for all delivered to the saints" (Jude 3). In other words, we need to care about orthodoxy and right thinking about who God is and how he saves through Jesus Christ. *Orthodoxy matters.*

But at the same time, God's Word commands us, "Love your neighbor as yourself" (Matthew 22:39). Jesus even told us, "Love your enemies" (Matthew 5:44). And 1 Peter 5:5

says, "Clothe yourselves, all of you, with humility toward one another, for 'God opposes the proud but gives grace to the humble.'" In other words, genuine love and humility of heart before God and other people are essential. *Humility matters.*

We don't get to choose between humility and orthodoxy. We need both.

IF NOT HUMBLE ORTHODOXY, THEN WHAT?

I know that humble orthodoxy sounds hard. In fact, it *is* hard. But ask yourself, what are the alternatives to humble orthodoxy?

> One of the mistakes Christians often make is that we learn to rebuke like Jesus but not love like Jesus.

I can think of two that are quite popular today.

To begin with, there's *arrogant orthodoxy.* It's possible to be right in our doctrine but be unkind and unloving, self-righteous and spiteful in our words and behavior.

If anyone thinks arrogant orthodoxy doesn't exist, he's never read the comments section of a Christian blog. One of the mistakes Christians often make is that we learn to rebuke like Jesus but not love like Jesus. Sometimes it seems that almost everyone who cares about doctrine is harsh and angry. Sadly, arrogant orthodoxy is the caricature that many people in our culture have of *any* Christian who has well-defined, strongly held biblical convictions.

Another popular option is *humble heterodoxy*. Heterodoxy is a departure from orthodoxy. So a person who is humbly heterodox abandons some of the historic Christian beliefs but is a really nice person who you'd enjoy having coffee with.

This is the person who can't bear to offend unbelievers or the general culture and seems open to almost any teaching in the name of inclusion, kindness, and open-mindedness. This approach avoids conflict. And it seems on the surface to be very gracious, even compassionate. But is it faithful? A song by Steve Taylor includes the line "You're so open-minded that your brain leaked out."[1] Well, some of us can so desire to appear humble that all our biblical faithfulness leaks out.

When I think about arrogant orthodoxy, I have to ask,

does good doctrine necessarily lead to being argumentative and arrogant?

And when I think about humble heterodoxy, my question is, do humility and kindness and engagement with our culture have to involve watering down our convictions?

I think the answer to both questions is no. We can—and we need to—embrace a *humble orthodoxy*. A letter written to a pastor can help us better understand both words in this term.

LAST TESTAMENT

He was young and afraid. What business did he have being a pastor? He wondered sometimes. How could he lead a church being torn by opposition? He wanted to be bold. He wanted to be fearless. He prayed that God would make him so. But he felt so isolated, so completely alone. And then the letter came. Its message must have hit him like a blow to the stomach, knocking the air out of him.

That letter is known today as 2 Timothy. The young pastor was Timothy. His friend, mentor, and father in the faith—the apostle Paul—was writing to say good-bye. "I am already being poured out as a drink offering," Paul wrote, "and the time of my departure has come" (4:6).

This time Paul wasn't going to be released from prison. He was going to be executed.

And what did he choose for his final message? Looking ahead to the future of the fledgling church, Paul's driving concern was the preservation of Christian orthodoxy. For Paul, this wasn't about proving someone else wrong, winning an argument, or adding people to his little club. For Paul, orthodoxy made the difference between life and death, heaven and hell. Whether or not it was faithfully communicated determined if the world would know the saving truth about Jesus Christ.

Paul urged Timothy to stand unashamed on the truth about Jesus's life, suffering, and bodily resurrection. "Remember Jesus Christ, risen from the dead, the offspring of David, as preached in my gospel," he wrote (2:8).

You might think that telling a Christian to "remember Jesus" borders on the unnecessary. Can Christians really forget him? Paul knew they could. And even worse, he knew they could claim allegiance to Jesus but lose sight of the real meaning of his life and death.

The true message of the gospel was under attack. False

teachers parading as Christians had denied it, distorted it, and twisted it to serve their own ends. Paul compared their teaching to gangrene—a disease that rots human flesh into a guacamole-colored open sore and is often remedied by amputation (2:17–18). For Paul, the analogy was no exaggeration. A distorted gospel rots the soul.

The only antidote for Timothy, said Paul, was to keep teaching the orthodox truths of the faith that had been passed down to him. "Follow the pattern of the sound words that you have heard from me, in the faith and love that are in Christ Jesus," Paul urged. "By the Holy Spirit who dwells within us, guard the good deposit entrusted to you" (1:13–14).

People often think of orthodoxy as lifeless and restrictive— a paint-by-numbers guide that stifles creativity. But Paul saw it as a treasure. It wasn't a canvas for self-expression; it was a "good deposit," something so precious that it needed to be guarded and protected.

Now it was Timothy's job to display the beauty of this treasure, to preserve it, and to pass it on unaltered to those who would follow. "What you have heard from me in the presence of many witnesses," Paul wrote, "entrust to faithful men who will be able to teach others also" (2:2).

Reading 2 Timothy reminds me of the sad reality of falsehood and lies. I wish I lived in a world where beliefs were like different flavors of ice cream—no wrong answers, just different options. But that's not the world we live in. We live in a world of truths and lies. We live in a world in which God's true revelation and the smooth words of charlatans and false prophets compete for our attention. A world where murder, genocide, human trafficking, and the worship of idols exist. A world where teachers and writers offer empty hope in human achievement and material possessions (3:1–9). A world filled with evil and an Evil One who is bent on distorting and destroying the truth and those who believe it (1 Peter 5:8).

Love for God and love for neighbor require us to oppose falsehood. There is nothing more unloving than to be silent in the face of lies that will ruin another person. Sometimes love demands that we say, "This philosophy, no matter how plausible or popular, is not true. This person, no matter how likable, gifted, or well intentioned, is teaching something that contradicts God's Word; therefore, it is untrue."

Paul was arguing for this type of love-infused courage— a courage that is willing to contend for God's unchanging truth.

> People often think of orthodoxy as lifeless
> and restrictive—a paint-by-numbers guide
> that stifles creativity. But Paul saw it as a
> treasure.

THE IMPORTANCE OF HOW

You and I need to contend for the truth. But there's a fine line
between contending for truth and being contentious. I think
this is why, in his final instructions to Timothy, the seasoned
apostle went out of his way to tell Timothy that even though
orthodoxy is important, it's not enough by itself.

Truth matters, but so does our attitude. We have to live
and speak and interact with others in a spirit of humility.
Paul wrote:

> Have nothing to do with foolish, ignorant con-
> troversies; you know that they breed quarrels.
> And the Lord's servant must not be quarrelsome
> but kind to everyone, able to teach, patiently

> enduring evil, correcting his opponents with
> gentleness. God may perhaps grant them repent-
> ance leading to a knowledge of the truth, and
> they may come to their senses and escape from
> the snare of the devil, after being captured by
> him to do his will. (2 Timothy 2:23–26)

I find these words amazing in light of Paul's circumstances. He was about to die. He saw false teachers working
to destroy the church. He had been betrayed and abandoned.
You would expect him to say, "Nuke the heretics, and don't
worry about civilian casualties!" But he didn't. Instead he
said, in effect, "Don't be a jerk."

Don't be quarrelsome. Don't get sidetracked on secondary issues. Be kind. Be patient. When other people are evil,
endure it while trusting in God. When you need to correct
someone, do it with gentleness.

Even when Paul was opposing false teachers—the enemies of orthodoxy—he hoped that his correction would
bring them to their senses. Maybe he recalled standing by as
Stephen was murdered (Acts 7:54–60). On that day no one
could have imagined that Saul, the destroyer of the church,

would become Paul, the defender of the church and an apostle of Christ Jesus. But the risen Lord had rescued him and commissioned him to announce the gospel across the world.

> Paul didn't just want to beat his opponents in an argument; he wanted to win them to the truth.

Paul had been shown grace by the Lord. So he did the same toward others, even opponents. He genuinely cared about people who disagreed with him. Even when he fiercely opposed them, he didn't just want to beat them in an argument; he wanted to win them to the truth.

100 PERCENT DEPENDENT ON GRACE

The letter of 2 Timothy, with its emphases on both orthodoxy and humility, is as relevant today as it has ever been. Maybe more so.

We live in a day when certainty is out of style. If you stand up and say, "I know that this is true and it's true for everyone," people will look at you and respond, "What's wrong with you? You're arrogant. Why would you want to foist that on me? Keep that to yourself."

It's so easy for us as Christians to bend to this mind-set. But we don't have the luxury or the biblical permission to be uncertain about those things God has been clear on. We haven't been asked to cut and paste God's truth to fit our tastes. That's why what we put in and what we leave out are so important. A pattern of sound words has been passed down to us and is now in our care.

And this is perfectly consistent with having the loving attitude toward others that Paul taught about and that Jesus embodied. Other people may react to the offense of the gospel with resistance from their sinful nature, but they are right to expect kindness from us. There's no reason for us to stand above them and preach down to them, condemning them as if we are somehow better than they.

When it comes to orthodoxy, it's not about you or me. The truth is not our truth; it comes from God. And the ability to uphold it with loving humility comes from him too.

As New Testament professor Michael Kruger asserts, "One can be certain and humble at the same time."

How? For this simple reason: Christians believe that they understand truth only because God has revealed it to them (1 Cor 1:26–30). In other words, Christians are humble because their understanding of truth is not based on their own intelligence, their own research, their own acumen. Rather, it is 100% dependent on the grace of God. Christian knowledge is a *dependent* knowledge. And that leads to humility (1 Cor 1:31). This obviously doesn't mean all Christians are personally humble. But, it does mean they should be, and have adequate grounds to be.[2]

Humble orthodoxy isn't easy. But with God's gracious help, through his Word and Spirit, you and I—and all our brothers and sisters in Christ—*can* live it out.

> We don't have the luxury or the biblical permission to be uncertain about those things God has been clear on.

2

With a Tear in Our Eye

Jesus once told a story about two men who went to pray. (You can read it in Luke 18.) His purpose for telling the story was to challenge people who trusted in their own righteousness and treated others with contempt. At the risk of coming across as irreverent (not at all what I intend), I'm going to take the liberty of retelling Jesus's parable to challenge those of us who trust in the rightness of our *doctrine* and look down on others.

One day two men went to church to pray.

The first man was a shallow, uninformed evangelical. Everything about him shouted of squishy theology. He didn't know or use big theological words. He watched Christian TV and thought it was deep. He bought books from the inspirational section of the bookstore. He attended one of those megachurches where the sermons are short and the worship leaders look like *American Idol* contestants.

The second man who went to pray was different. He was a Christian of theological depth and substance—this was obvious by the heavy study Bible he carried with him. He only read books by long-dead theologians. He subscribed to the podcasts of all the solid, gospel-centered expository preachers who didn't tell funny stories or make jokes in their sermons. He felt cheated if a sermon was less than an hour long.

This second man began to pray. He said, "God, I thank you that I am not like other people—doctrinally ignorant, theologically clueless, superficial in their saccharine-sweet evangelicalism. I thank you that you have made me what I am: true to good doctrine, uncompromising on teaching, orthodox to the core."

But the first man would not even look up to heaven. Instead he beat his breast and said, "God, have mercy on me, a sinner."

If you consider yourself a person who takes doctrine seriously, do you see yourself in this story? Has a humble gratefulness for God's mercy been replaced by a pride in all that you know? Are you prone to have contempt or a sense of superiority toward those with less knowledge? I believe Jesus would confront our misplaced confidence just as he did the self-righteousness of the Pharisees in his day.

In hymnist John Newton's words, we are great sinners who have a great Savior. We've been forgiven so much and have nothing in ourselves to be proud of. How then can we be modern-day Pharisees? Instead of looking down on the unorthodox, how can we not want to humbly lead them toward the same life-giving truth that has changed our lives?

MERCY RECIPIENTS

The message of Christian orthodoxy isn't that I'm right and someone else is wrong. It's that I am wrong and yet God is filled with grace. I am wrong, and yet God has made a way for me to be forgiven and accepted and loved for eternity. I am wrong, and yet God gave his Son, Jesus, to die in my place and receive my punishment. I am wrong, but through faith in Jesus, I can be made right before a holy God.

This is the gospel. This is the truth that all Christian doctrine celebrates. This is the truth that every follower of Jesus Christ is called to cherish and preserve. Even die for. It is the only truth on which we can build our lives and rest our eternal hope.

The gospel was at the heart of Paul's thinking when he wrote about guarding the good deposit and instructing others gently. And likewise it should be at the heart of what we do. We teach the truth because the gospel is at stake. We live the truth because the gospel has changed us. And we represent the truth humbly because we hope the same gospel that has rescued us will rescue other people.

How can we be arrogant about a truth that is completely outside of anything we've done? If we had earned the gospel, we could be arrogant about it. If we had somehow created the truth, then we could copyright it and control other people's access to it. But the truth is a gift from God to us. It has changed us only because he extended his mercy to us. How then can we not extend mercy to others?

Sound doctrine is vital. Godly example is essential. But

they are not enough. Apart from humility of heart, we will be like the Pharisees and will use the truth as a stick to beat other people over the head. And God will be dishonored in that. If we would honor God, we must represent truth humbly in our words, in our demeanor, and in our attitude.

It's not that we're gentle and patient and kind because we're slaves to public opinion. We are to humbly deliver the truth because we are slaves to Christ. We are servants of the one who humbled himself even unto death on a cross. And when his enemies pinned his hands to that tree with nails, he did not fight back.

> The message of Christian orthodoxy isn't that I'm right and someone else is wrong. It's that I am wrong and yet God is filled with grace.

When you truly understand the doctrine of grace in the gospel, you don't go around checking people's IDs to see if they are in or out. You walk around with tears of gratefulness in your eyes, saying, "Why in the world would he choose me?" And with love in your heart toward those who are still lost, you yearn for them to receive the same miracle of undeserved forgiveness.

Our view of who we are in relation to our holy God makes all the difference. That's what the great general Joshua learned in a curious encounter he had on the eve of battle.

WHAT DOES THE LORD SAY?

As the successor to Moses, Joshua had crossed the Jordan River with the people of Israel to take possession of the land God had promised to their forefather Abraham hundreds of years before. Now he was facing the collective resistance of the Canaanite peoples who were entrenched in the land. Naturally enough, Joshua probably felt trepidation. The thought in his mind was likely, *Is God going to back us in this thing?*

Then he had a strange encounter with a sword-wielding man called "the commander of the army of the LORD" (Joshua 5:14). There is some mystery about who this figure was, whether an angel of the Lord or, as many believe, the Lord himself—an appearance of the preincarnate Christ.

But before Joshua found out who this armed man was, he strode right up to him and asked, "Are you for us, or for our adversaries?" (verse 13). It's an understandable question, isn't it? Joshua was about to start a war in enemy territory, and suddenly he found an armed man standing in front of him. He needed to know if this person was friend or foe.

The problem is that we often ask the same question of God. We want him to declare himself as being on *our side*. We tell ourselves that we're fighting for orthodoxy and for biblical faithfulness, but in subtle ways our heart struggle becomes about our identity, our rightness, our purity, our truth. And it becomes less and less about who God is and his glory and his name.

I love the way the commander of the Lord's army answered Joshua's question. Joshua had asked, "Are you for us, or for our adversaries?" The heavenly general replied, "No; but I am the commander of the army of the LORD. Now I have come" (verse 14).

No.

Essentially he was saying, "God is not on *your* side. You'd better get on *his* side."

God doesn't need any of us. God is building his church,

and it will prevail. His Word endures forever. He laughs at the nations. No vote can be taken that can push him out of power. God is God. We'd better get on his side.

Joshua got it. He fell on his face and worshiped God. That's the posture of humble orthodoxy—on your face before God, worshiping him for who he is. We stop saying, "God, won't you endorse my position?" and we start saying, "God, this is about you. You are the glorious one. You are to be praised. I want to live my life for your fame."

God's truth isn't ours in the sense that it exists for building our kingdom. God's truth is his, and it is for his glory and his worship. He doesn't sign on to our agenda. We sign on to his. We bow to him.

> God doesn't sign on to our agenda. We sign on to his.

So the right question isn't "Are you for us, or for our adversaries?" Rather, we should be asking the question Joshua asked of the angel: "What does my lord say to his servant?" (verse 14). And the answer Joshua received was that he should worship with even greater reverence. Joshua was already on his knees. The commander of the army of the Lord instructed him to take off his shoes so that he could esteem God more and worship him better.

That must always be the driving passion behind our pursuit of biblical orthodoxy. Not to prove ourselves more right or better than someone else but to better worship the holy God, the one who forgives and accepts us for Christ's sake alone.

THE TINY KINGDOM OF SELF

So, if we've received overwhelming mercy through no agency of our own, why do so many of us who care about right doctrine have a harsh streak? Why are so many theology-loving Christians intent on building up their own kingdoms instead of getting on the side of the King of heaven and worshiping him? Why is there so much arrogant orthodoxy in the church?

The Bible says that "'knowledge' puffs up, but love builds up" (1 Corinthians 8:1). Ever since the first man and woman in the garden turned from God to gain the sweet, forbidden knowledge offered by the serpent, every human heart has been plagued by an inclination to pursue knowledge to inflate self rather than to glorify God.

In his book *The Reason for God,* Tim Keller says that all sin is an attempt to find a sense of identity and meaning apart from God. "So, according to the Bible," he writes, "the primary way to define sin is not just the doing of bad things, but the making of good things into *ultimate* things."[3]

> If being right becomes more important to us than worshiping God, then our theology is not really about God anymore. It's about us.

Applied to the topic at hand, Keller's point is that if we make a good thing like correct theology the ultimate end—if being right becomes more important to us than worshiping God—then our theology is not really about God anymore. It's about us. It becomes the source of our sense of worth and identity. And if theology becomes about us, then we'll despise and demonize those who oppose us.[4]

Knowledge about God that doesn't translate into exalting

him in our words, thoughts, and actions will soon become self-exaltation. And then we'll attack anyone who threatens our tiny Kingdom of Self.

If we stand before the awesome knowledge of God's character and our first thought isn't *I am small, and I am unworthy to know the Creator of the universe,* then we should be concerned. Too many of us catch a glimpse of him and think, *Look at me, taking all this in. Think of all the poor fools who have never seen this. God, you're certainly lucky to have me beholding you.*

Pastor Greg Dutcher says, "We cross a line when we are more focused on mastering theology than on being mastered by Christ."[5] How easy it is to cross that line.

HUMILITY WITH COMPASSION

It's regrettable that human sin can distort sound teaching just as it can mess up anything else that's good in the world. But should this cause us to abandon the pursuit and defense of biblical truth? Paul didn't think so. He spent some of his last moments of life urging Timothy to hold to the truth about Jesus. And the problems of pride and turf wars wouldn't go away even if we tried to avoid orthodoxy. We'd just find something else to throw at each other. We'd find something else to be proud about.

We have to commit ourselves to holding on to the truth *and* never giving up on showing love to others.

Francis Schaeffer, a Christian writer and thinker from the previous century, modeled this kind of humility with compassion. He genuinely loved people. And even as he analyzed and critiqued the culture, he did so "with a tear in his eye."[6]

That is humble orthodoxy. It's standing for truth with a tear in our eye. It's assuring a friend living in sexual sin that we love her even as we tell her that her sexual activity is disobedient to God. It's remembering that angry, unkind opponents of the gospel are human beings created in the image of God who need the same mercy he has shown us. It's remembering that when we're arrogant and self-righteous in the way we represent orthodoxy, our lives contradict what we claim to believe.

But while we shouldn't be mean and spiteful in representing biblical truth, neither should we apologize for believing that God has been clear in his Word. The humility we need in our theology is first and foremost a humility before God. As Pastor Mark Dever puts it, "Humble theology [is] theology which submits itself to the truth of God's Word."[7] This is a good reminder for me. Because I think it's possible for me (or anyone for that matter) to overreact to arrogant orthodoxy with a brand of squishy theology, believing others are arrogant if they think the Bible teaches anything clearly.

> Genuine orthodoxy—the heart of which is the death of God's Son for undeserving sinners—is the most humbling, human-pride-smashing message in the world.

Truth can be known. And what the Bible teaches should be obeyed. Just because we can't know God exhaustively doesn't mean we can't know him truly (Psalm 19:7–10; John 17:17). Just because there is mystery in God's Word doesn't mean we can pretend God hasn't spoken clearly in the Bible.

"Christian humility," Dever writes, "is to simply accept whatever God has revealed in His Word. Humility is following God's Word wherever it goes, as far as it goes, not either going beyond it or stopping short of it.... The humility we want in our churches is to read the Bible and believe it.... It is not humble to be hesitant where God has been clear and plain."[8]

The solution to arrogant orthodoxy, then, is not less orthodoxy. It's more.

Genuine orthodoxy—the heart of which is the death of God's Son for undeserving sinners—is the most humbling, human-pride-smashing message in the world. And if we truly know the gospel of grace, it will create in us a heart of humility and grace toward others.

3

Repentance Starts with Me

Justin lives in Chicago. At six foot two, he's about twice as tall as I am. He's at least that much smarter as well. God has given Justin a sharp mind, and he loves to use it to think about and delight in God's truth. His latest project at his job was to work with more than ninety Bible scholars to create a new (and I would say amazing) study Bible.

On the side Justin also runs a blog that covers a wide array of theological and cultural topics. Called *Between Two Worlds,* it has become one of the most popular Christian sites on the Internet.[9] And as a result it often becomes a battle-ground for Christians from different backgrounds and de-nominations. The comments can get ugly and personal. And frequently Justin is the target.

Many times I've watched Justin respond to angry words with kindness. I've heard him pray for people who are misrepresenting him and watched him resist the urge to strike back.

Justin cares about truth, but he's gracious toward those he disagrees with. He reaches out to Christians who differ with him on points of doctrine. He listens to them. He never budges in his commitment to orthodoxy, but he stands his ground with genuine humility. And when he encounters hate, he refuses to hate back.

Like any genuinely humble person, Justin is uncomfortable being held up as a paragon of humility. But it means a lot to me that he gave me permission to talk about him in this context. You see, in important ways, Justin has helped me understand the causal relationship between humility and orthodoxy. As he puts it, humility leads to orthodoxy, and orthodoxy leads to humility. Think about that. If we're truly humble, we'll acknowledge that we need truth from God. We won't think that we can invent or create our own ideas about who God is. Humility will lead us to accept God's words and his explanation for the world and our need for salvation. And in the same way, if we truly know and embrace orthodoxy, it should humble us. When we know the truth about God— his love, his power, his greatness, his holiness, his mercy—it doesn't leave us boasting. It leaves us amazed. It leaves us in awe of truth. It leaves us humbled in the presence of grace.

Though I'm not fully there yet, deep down that's where I yearn to be. And even that desire, I believe, comes as a gift from God.

As a matter of fact, all of us should be less concerned with whether others are being faithful to God's truth than with whether *we* are being faithful to God. One of the best biblical guides for this attitude is an Old Testament king you may not have thought about in a while: Josiah.

Causal relationship: humility leads to ortho-doxy, and orthodoxy leads to humility.

A ROBE TORN

Josiah lived more than six hundred years before Christ. By the time Josiah came along, the people of Judah had been in rebellion against God for a long time. They still had the temple, and they went through the motions of being religious, but their lives were filled with idolatry and immorality, injustice and oppression.

The incredible thing is that, decades before, the priests had actually misplaced the scroll containing the law of God. So for all that time the nation hadn't been hearing from the Lord through his written commands. But then one day, after King Josiah had ordered that the temple be renovated, someone happened to find the long-lost scroll.

Josiah's reaction when he had the Book of the Law read to him and found out how far his people had drifted from obedience to God was exemplary. He could have started blaming those who were less godly than he. He could have delivered punishments to those who had violated the newly rediscovered laws. But he did none of this. What *did* he do? He tore his clothes and wept before the Lord (2 Kings 22:10–11, 19). In his culture that was a way of humbling oneself. Josiah was saying, "*I* have done wrong. The repentance needs to start with *me*."

This is just the kind of humility we need today. Orthodoxy shouldn't be a club to attack someone else. It should be a double-edged sword that starts by piercing our hearts, laying them bare before God so that we say, "Forgive *us*, Lord!"

G. K. Chesterton wrote in his book *Orthodoxy*, "What we suffer from to-day is humility in the wrong place. Modesty has moved from the organ of ambition. Modesty has settled upon the organ of conviction; where it was never meant to be. A man was meant to be doubtful about himself, but undoubting about the truth."[10] In other words, we need humility about our own failings in light of God's Word, not a humility that doubts the clarity, authority, and sufficiency of Scripture.

One test for whether we're pursuing humble orthodoxy is this question: Are we giving as much energy to obeying and being reformed by God's Word *personally* as we are to criticizing its detractors?

It's easy to take shots at television preachers who promote a health-and-wealth gospel. But am I allowing the Word to correct my own materialistic heart that often wants God's blessings more than it wants him? Am I being reformed by the Word, which calls me to deny myself and take up my cross and follow him (Mark 8:34)?

It's easy to critique authors who deny the existence of hell. But am I allowing the Bible's difficult doctrine of God's wrath toward sinners to reshape my life and priorities so

that I pray, give, and sacrifice to see the gospel reach un-
believing people in this world? As Pastor David Platt has
said, many of us in the church have embraced a functional
universalism that is more concerned with our comforts than
with the eternal destiny of those who haven't heard the good
news.[11]

> Are we giving as much energy to obeying
> God's Word *personally* as we are to criti-
> cizing its detractors?

Shouldn't individuals and churches that hold most faithfully to orthodoxy and biblical truth be the most frequently
filled with godly repentance?

Shouldn't we be known for consistent confession of all
the ways our own lives fall short of the truth we espouse?

Shouldn't the watching world be able to see not only our
condemnation of false teaching but also our tears and cries
for mercy because of our own errors?

We all have good cause to tear our robes.

LIVING IT

I won't pretend that I've arrived at humble orthodoxy. When I gain a bit of theological knowledge, I all too frequently get puffed up with pride. But I'll tell you what deflates my arrogance and self-righteousness faster than anything else: trying to live whatever truth I have.

God's Word insists that we can't merely know and teach truth; we must embody it. We have to apply it to our lives. We must submit ourselves to the authority of Scripture and the claims of the gospel not merely intellectually but also in our thoughts, in our careers, in our relationships. Truth that is divorced from personal practice is hypocrisy, and living truth becomes a living lie when we fail to obey it ourselves.

Do you want to keep your orthodoxy humble? Try to live it. Don't spend all your time theorizing about it, debating it, or blogging about it. Spend more energy living the truth you know than worrying about what the next person does or doesn't know. Don't measure yourself by what you know. Measure yourself by your practice of what you know.

Do I know something of the doctrine of God? Can I list his attributes of sovereignty, omnipotence, and love? Then I should live that truth and stop worrying and complaining and being anxious.

Do I know something of the doctrine of justification? Can I tell you that I'm justified by grace alone through faith alone in Christ alone? Good. Then I should live that truth by repenting of my worthless efforts to earn God's approval. I should weep over my self-righteousness when I think and act toward others as if I'm anything but the recipient of pure, unmerited grace.

Do I know something about the doctrine of sanctification? Do I know the priority of holiness and the reality of remaining sin in my life? Then why attack or look down on another Christian who seems less sanctified? I have enough areas where I need to grow to keep me busy. I should pray for more of the Holy Spirit's power to enable me to advance in obedience.

I think this is what Paul was telling Timothy to do when he said, "Watch your life and doctrine closely. Persevere in them, because if you do, you will save both yourself and your hearers" (1 Timothy 4:16, NIV). It's not enough to get our doctrine straight. Life and doctrine can't be separated. Our lives either put the beauty of God's truth on display, or they obscure it.

> Don't measure yourself by what you know. Measure yourself by your practice of what you know.

We can't afford to grow casual toward our own propensity to sin. Even the great leader Moses let his guard down and earned God's displeasure by allowing the disobedience of others to lead him into his own disobedience.

REBELLIOUS LEADER OF A REBELLIOUS PEOPLE

Moses and the people of Israel were in the Sinai Desert, and they ran out of water. They started complaining to their leader, "Why have you brought the assembly of the LORD into this wilderness, that we should die here, both we and our cattle? And why have you made us come up out of Egypt to bring us to this evil place? It is no place for grain or figs

or vines or pomegranates, and there is no water to drink"
(Numbers 20:4–5).

Annoyed with these grumblers yet also understanding
the need for water, Moses asked the Lord what to do.

The Lord told him to assemble all the people and "tell
the rock before their eyes to yield its water" (verse 8).

So Moses took the people (whom he called "rebels") to a
rock and struck the rock twice with his staff (verses 10–11).
The text doesn't fully explain what was taking place in Moses's
heart, but what seems evident is that when Moses struck the
rock, an energy and a passion were motivating him that had
nothing to do with the glory of God. He appears to have
been more concerned with vindicating himself, more preoccupied with the waywardness of the people than with the
holiness of God.

Despite this, God was faithful to his promise. Sufficient
water came out to meet all the people's present needs.

The people were happy.

Moses finally may have been happy.

But the Lord wasn't happy.

You see, Moses hadn't strictly obeyed his instructions.
The Lord had told him to *tell* the rock to yield water. Instead,

Moses, in his anger against the grumbling people of Israel, *struck* the rock. So God chastised Moses: "You did not believe in me, to uphold me as holy in the eyes of the people of Israel" (verse 12).

I don't know about you, but I want to give Moses a pass on this one. His seemingly minor trespass pales in comparison to the outrageous behavior of the people he led.

> Even when people in our culture are sinning, slandering, and tearing down truth, I have no excuse for ignoring God's commands.

Think about the Israelites: They were quarreling with God's chosen prophet. They and their parents had tested God over and over again. After being rescued from slavery, they wanted to turn back to Egypt. They worshiped the golden calf. They refused to go into the Promised Land. Whenever they faced any trouble, they instantly began to gripe, complain, and speak of rebellion. These opponents and detractors of Moses were wrong through and through—wrong in their beliefs and sinful in their actions.

Yet even this blatant, wicked rebellion did not justify the slightest disobedience to God on Moses's part. And that disobedience equaled a lost opportunity to highlight God's holiness.

Here's the point: the error and sin of others never give me license to ignore the Word of God. Even when people in our culture are sinning, slandering, and tearing down truth, I have no excuse for ignoring God's commands. Their sin doesn't give me a pass to sin.

Let's take a warning from this story and be sobered. No matter how wrong someone else is, God is always evaluating my heart and yours. And if we regard him as holy, we will never lose sight of that. We will never lose sight of him or of our duty to him.

MEMORIES OF THE "CAGE STAGE"

I heard someone describe people who have just discovered the importance of sound doctrine as being in the "cage stage." In other words, they should be caged because their newfound zeal for truth often makes them dangerous, even vicious, in their self-righteousness and criticism of others whom they deem less informed.

I went through my own cage stage in my early twenties. I was introduced to the beautiful truths of God's sovereignty in my salvation, of justification by faith alone, and the priority of sanctification—of growing to be more like Christ in my words and deeds. It was thrilling to see more of who God is and how he'd acted in Christ to save me. I made new friends who shared the same love for biblical truth and who helped me grow in my knowledge.

But in subtle ways my heart wasn't feeding only on truth; it was also feeding on a sense of superiority. I didn't just have truth. I had truth other people lacked. I wasn't just looking up and beholding God's glory. I was looking down on others.

When I would attend a conference or be in some teaching setting where members of different denominations or Christian groups were present, I'd take time afterward to reflect on what I'd learned. Sadly, what I'd "learned" was usually how grateful I was that I knew better than these fellow Christians. In the name of discernment, I'd criticize aspects of their theology, their practice, and their emphasis.

I have a genuine sense of sadness as I look back on my attitude in so many of those discussions, because I know I wasn't pleasing the Lord. It wasn't passion for his name and his truth that was guiding me in those moments. It was a smug sense of self-satisfaction in being better informed than someone else.

Is there an important place for exercising discernment? Absolutely. And shouldn't we evaluate carefully the teaching and the practices at conferences and in books and other material? No question. But as author Trevin Wax points out, there's a difference between having a critical mind that carefully evaluates and having a critical spirit that loves to tear down and belittle.[12] Too often I've been guilty of having a critical spirit.

> There's a difference between having a critical mind that carefully evaluates and having a critical spirit that loves to tear down.

In the past five years, God has patiently adjusted my attitude. Hebrews 12:5–11 says that God our Father disciplines us because he loves us. He brings circumstances, even pain, into our lives to shake out of our hands "every weight" and the "sin which clings so closely" (verse 1). I had pride and a sense of superiority. I thought my truth and my practices were better than other people's. And God used some painful circumstances to humble me. He took me down a notch or two (or three) in my own estimation.

And do you know what? Being humbled like that was the best thing that ever happened to me.

Today in new ways I see grace in other denominations and ministries. I can better learn from other people instead of feeling the need to protect myself by showing why I'm more right than they are. And I'm more ready to extend grace and understanding toward those who are still in process, just as I am.

That's the way it is with humble orthodoxy. Others may have specks in their eyes, but we've got logs in ours (Matthew 7:1–5). So humility doesn't start with someone else. It always begins at our own address.

And in the end it leads to the approval of God. Let me tell you what I mean.

4

Living for God's Approval

Sadly, many people in our day treat truth more like a personal accessory than a life-defining reality. For them, truth is like a pair of jeans they pick out. *I sort of like that doctrine,* they might think. *And I'll identify myself with this teaching here because I want to be that kind of person. But that teaching over there? Forget about it!* It's not really a matter of wrestling with truth and having deep convictions. It's just picking and choosing and making a statement about themselves.

> Truth is not about us. It is about God.

I'll give you another comparison.

Have you ever gone online and checked out celebrity playlists? These are lists where famous people—actors, musicians, comedians, or whoever—tell you the songs they like. You wonder if they (or their publicists) put a lot of time into picking these songs, not really because they have strong feelings about the music itself, but because they want you to look at their list of songs and think something like this: *Whoa, this person's really distinguished. He's eclectic in his tastes. He loves good music, but he also has a fun sensibility.*

Nobody wants to put up a playlist that says, "I'm really into [insert name of the latest pop diva]. She just rocks it." No, they want to be impressive. Most of all, they want you to know they are aware of music you have never heard of. Their playlist has to say, "Only two people on the planet are aware of this band. I am one of them, okay?"

Sometimes that's the way people approach doctrine and truth. They want to dip into something because it's kind of edgy, because it's the new thing, because it makes a statement about them.

Friend, the truth is not about us. It's not self-determined. It's not an accessory. It is about God. And we believe it and we hold to it, not because we want to make a statement about ourselves, but because we want true statements to be made about him. We want his glory.

That's why we must realize that the truth is bigger than we are. And that's why we must think about how we are going to relate to it now and for the rest of our lives. Even forever.

WHOSE APPROVAL?

Follow the pattern of sound words, Paul said in 2 Timothy. Guard the good deposit that was entrusted to you (1:13–14).

But at the same time, have nothing to do with foolish, ignorant controversies that breed quarrels. Instead be kind to everyone, able to teach, patiently enduring evil, correcting opponents with gentleness in the hope that God may grant them repentance leading to a knowledge of the truth (2:23–25).

That's humble orthodoxy.

But along with all this, I want to point out one last thing from Paul's letter. He said to Timothy, "Do your best to present yourself to God as one approved, a worker who has no need to be ashamed, rightly handling the word of truth" (2:15).

Paul told Timothy to live for God's approval. Whose approval are *we* living for? And what do we have to do to get it?

You might not realize this, but right now our generation of Christians is wrestling with some big questions. What will the church look like in the coming years? Who is going to chart our course? What is our foundation going to be? What is going to guide our decisions? What is going to define us and motivate us? What are we to carry forward from the past, and what do we have the liberty to change? There's a real debate taking place.

Now, there's always a need for innovation and new ideas and change in methodology to proclaim the gospel more effectively. But the conversation that's taking place in our generation is going beyond mere methodology or practice. It's not about how we can be more effective in evangelism. Really, the conversation is about whether we can reinvent theology and belief.

And I believe at the heart of this conversation is the question, whose approval are we going to live for?

All of us who call ourselves by the name Christian know that we're *supposed* to live for God's approval. But it's so easy to get sidetracked. I can think of three ways Christian people are living for the approval of someone other than God.

First, many Christians today seem preoccupied with the

past generation and what they did or didn't do right. And so instead of living for the approval of God, they are busy reacting to people who have already gone on. It's a dangerous thing to react to something besides God's Word. It can so easily cause people to swerve from biblical priorities.

Next, some Christians, driven by a desire to reach lost people, cross the line from trying to reach our culture and start trying to impress our culture. And when a person is motivated by the desire to impress this fallen culture, very quickly all that God has to say becomes, instead of a precious truth, a hindrance. The Christians who go this way become slaves to the trends, to the values, to the ideals of a spiritually lost culture.

> It's a dangerous thing to react to something besides God's Word.

Finally, some Christians make the opposite mistake from the last one: they turn their back on culture altogether. They lock themselves in their little Christian subculture, move into their little Christian ghetto, and make their focus impressing other people within their little Christian clique. They might love truth, but to them truth isn't about God changing lost people; it's about them proving themselves right on any given issue.

I've been guilty of each of these three mistakes at different times and in different ways. In fact, I find it easy to bounce from one of these reactions to another like a steel ball in a pinball machine. Maybe you have found the same thing.

And that's why we need 2 Timothy 2:15.

We should do our best to present ourselves for approval— not to our place in history, not to our culture, not to our Christian peers, but to God. We are his servants. Only his approval matters.

We will only stand before him on the Last Day unashamed if we rightly handle the word of truth.

RIGHT HANDLING

The "word of truth" that Paul refers to in 2 Timothy 2:15 is simply the gospel—that God's Son took on our humanity, that he perfectly obeyed God's law, and that he laid down his life at Calvary for our sins and rose from the dead so we could be forgiven and accepted by God.

Will we rightly handle the gospel—passing it down unchanged as it was passed down to us? Or will we mishandle it?

The reason Paul was so committed to this matter was, first and foremost, for the glory of God. But it was also because he deeply loved and cared for people. So much of what motivated Paul—the reason he opposed false teachers, the reason he was willing to name the names of these false teachers (even in this passage)—was because he knew that false teaching deceives people and ruins souls for eternity. And we must understand this if we're going to grasp the importance of rightly handling the truth.

If somebody gives you a basketball and says, "Hey, rightly handle this basketball," you're not going to be too worried about dropping it, are you? After all, what happens when you drop a ball? It comes right back to you.

But if you're holding something that, if dropped, could explode and harm others, you're going to handle it with great care. You're going to be very concerned about rightly handling it.

When we mishandle the gospel, it's not like a ball that's just going to bounce back: "Oh, it turns out Jesus is divine, despite what I was saying. Well, no big deal." Or "So Jesus really is the only way to the Father. I sort of missed it on that one. Whatever."

No. Paul was pointing out that when the truth is mishandled, when falsehood is taught, it's not okay. It won't just work itself out. It destroys people's lives.

> If you're holding something that, if dropped, could explode and harm others, you're going to handle it with great care.

It's in this context that Paul discussed not quarreling about words. He was *not* discouraging commitment to the truth or precision about theology. He was *not* saying to be reticent in the fight for sound doctrine. Rather, he wanted Timothy to avoid controversy that distracts from the gospel. Paul was saying, "Don't get involved in all these squabbles that have nothing to do with the central truths of the message we've been given. Don't get sidetracked."

Essentially, what Paul was urging us to embrace is the right teaching—the orthodoxy—handed down by the apostles. And doing that is beautifully united with a humility of spirit. It all goes to the same end of honoring God as we serve his people.

APOLOGIES IN HEAVEN

Something that helps me in my pursuit of humble orthodoxy is to remember that one day in heaven there will be only one right person.

It won't be me. And I'm sorry to say so, but it won't be you either. It will be God. Everybody else in heaven will be wrong in a million different ways about a million different things. The Bible tells us that only those who trusted in Jesus Christ, who turned from sin and believed in him, will be in God's presence. But on a host of secondary matters, we'll all discover how much we got wrong.

Maybe some people picture heaven as a place where all the "right" people celebrate that they made it. But I don't think that's true. I think it will be a place of beautiful humility.

The funny thing is, I'm really looking forward to this aspect of heaven. I can't wait for that crystal-clear awareness of all the opinions and attitudes and ideas and strategies that I had in this life that were quite simply wrong.

No one will be proud. No one will be bragging. We all will want to talk about how wrong we were about so many things and how kind God was to us. I can imagine someone saying, "Seriously, I am the most unworthy person here."

And then someone else will say, "No, friend, it took more grace for me to be here. You need to hear my story."

And we'll say, "No offense, King David, but we've already heard your story. Let somebody else share." (Of course we'll let him share again later.)

At the end of every conversation, we'll agree that when we were back on the old earth, we had no idea how unmerited that grace really was. We called it grace, but we didn't really think it was totally grace. We thought we'd added just a tad of something good. That we had earned just a bit. We'll realize to our shame that to differing degrees we trusted in our intellect, our morality, the rightness of our doctrine, and our religious performance when all along it was completely grace.

"For by grace you have been saved through faith. And this is not your own doing; it is the gift of God, not a result of works, so that no one may boast" (Ephesians 2:8–9).

Every one of us will have a lot to apologize for.

I estimate that around the first ten thousand years of

heaven will be taken up with the redeemed people of God apologizing to each other for all the ways we judged each other, jostled for position, were proud and divisive and arrogant toward each other. (This is just an estimate. It could be the first twenty thousand years.)

I imagine Paul telling Barnabas he's sorry for splitting up the team over Mark. And Paul admitting to Mark how he should have been more willing to give him another chance. And then all the Christians from first-century Corinth will tell Paul how badly they feel about what a complete pain they were for him.

> Maybe some people picture heaven as a place where all the "right" people celebrate that they made it. But I don't think that's true.

All the people in churches who split over silly things like organ music will come together and hug each other. The Baptists and Presbyterians will get together, and one side will have to admit to the other side that they were wrong about baptism. And then the side that was right will say they're sorry for their pride and all the snide comments they made. And then there will be no more sides, and the whole thing will be forgotten.

Because of course we'll all be happy to forgive each other. And we'll keep saying, "But God used it for good. We couldn't see it then, but he was at work even in our weakness and sin."

TRUTH FOREVER VINDICATED

In eternity we'll see the silliness of self-righteousness and quarreling over the nonessentials. But we'll also see with piercing clarity just how essential the essentials really are. We'll see just how precious the truths of the gospel really are.

We will look into each other's eyes, and we won't be able to stop saying, "It was all true! It was all true!" Every word. Every promise.

We'll see that the Cross really did conquer death and hell and wash away our sins. We'll see the everlasting reward of believing in Jesus and the eternal hell of rejecting him. We'll look back on our lives and see that God never did forsake us. Not even for a split second. That he was with us every moment—even the darkest moments of despair and seeming hopelessness. We will know in a deeper way than we can now imagine that God truly worked all things together for our good. And we'll see that Jesus really did go to prepare a place for us, just as he said.

And everything we did for the sake of Jesus will be so worth it. Every time we stood for truth and looked foolish. Every time we shared the gospel. Every act of service. Every sacrifice.

> In eternity no one will say, "I wish I'd believed less. I wish I'd cared less about the gospel."

We will meet men and women from every nation of the old earth who gave their lives for the cause of the gospel— martyrs who died rather than abandon the unchanging truths of the faith. We'll meet people who lost homes and family and whose bodies were whipped and tortured and burned because they refused to renounce the name of Jesus. And we will honor them, and all will see that what they lost and suffered was nothing in comparison to what they gained.

When that day comes, no one will say, "I wish I'd believed

less. I wish I'd cared less about the glory of Jesus Christ. I wish I'd cared less about the gospel."

In the meantime, we should strive to hold our beliefs with a charity and kindness that won't embarrass us in heaven.

FAITHFUL NO MATTER WHAT

I can imagine someone saying, "Okay, humble orthodoxy sounds good. I'm sure I'll look back from heaven and wish I'd been more humble in my orthodoxy and more orthodox in my humility. But if I try to live this way now, will the world notice? Will it help people to accept the gospel message? Will it advance the cause of Christ?

"Does humble orthodoxy *work*?"

I think the answer is yes. And no.

The answer is yes in that, if we live with a heart of compassion and humility, the Holy Spirit can use that to draw people to God. Our behavior can "adorn the doctrine of God our Savior" (Titus 2:10).

But the answer is also no. Remember that Paul wrote 2 Timothy from prison near the end of his life. He had been abandoned by most of his friends. He was about to be executed. Obviously his own humility in defending orthodox truth had not prevented his opponents from hounding him to his very death. This means that humble orthodoxy doesn't necessarily work if our goal is acceptance, respect, and admiration from this world.

> Humble orthodoxy matters because God's truth matters and because the reality of God's character must shape ours.

The gospel is and always will be offensive to sinners. People will still follow false teachers no matter how humble and kind we are. Fundamentally, it's not the packaging the world doesn't like. Sinful people hate the gospel itself. False teachers will still thrive and gain their followings and, to add insult to injury, will be better liked than we are.

But that's not the point. Humble orthodoxy is not a technique to win a following. That's not why it matters.

It matters because God's truth matters and because the reality of God's character must shape ours. We must be ready to suffer for the truth of God's Word and still be gracious and compassionate. We must be humble even as we contend for the truth and seem to be losing. God hasn't commanded us to win. He has told us to trust him and do as he has taught. This is how we receive his approval.

We're going to be opposed as we preach substitutionary atonement and the truth of God's wrath toward sin. We're going to look unloving and unkind as we teach God's plan for marriage being one man and one woman. We're not going to look cool. We're going to look ridiculous and backward and intolerant and politically incorrect to the world.

Here's the question: As we lose the esteem of our culture, as we see false teachers gaining ground, what will we do? Will we grow bitter, angry, and vengeful? Or, like Jesus and Paul, will we continue to love our enemies even as we suffer? Will we keep praying? Will we keep hoping for God to open others' eyes?

We don't have to be jerks with the truth. We can remember how Jesus showed us mercy when we were his enemies. We can demonstrate a humble orthodoxy, holding on to our identity in the gospel. We are not those who are right; we are those who have been redeemed.

Study Guide

4 Sections for Individual or Group Use

SECTION 1
Your Attitude Matters

Some people love biblical doctrine but are annoying, argumentative, and arrogant. Others are likable and inoffensive folks who consider themselves to have license in choosing which of the historic Christian doctrines they will embrace. But what if God wants us to care about godly truth *and* treat other people with loving-kindness? The fact is, he does. And that's called *humble orthodoxy.* God, through his Spirit and his Word, enables us to hold on to both humility and right belief about him.

Questions

1. What's your first reaction when someone uses the word *orthodoxy*? What past experiences in your life

helped to determine your response to this term and the concept of right thinking about God?

2. What's your first reaction to the concept of humble orthodoxy? What relevance does this topic have to your life today?

3. The following boxes are obviously oversimplified. Still, when you look at them, what people or incidents come to mind? Which box do you think most accurately describes *you*? Why?

1 Arrogant heterodoxy (bad doctrine, bad behavior)	2 Arrogant orthodoxy (good doctrine, bad behavior)
3 Humble heterodoxy (bad doctrine, good behavior)	4 Humble orthodoxy (good doctrine, good behavior)

4. Get out your Bible, and carefully read all four chapters of 2 Timothy, looking for statements from the apostle Paul emphasizing (a) that ortho-doxy matters and (b) that humility matters. If you want, use pens or highlighters in two different col-ors to mark the twin emphases in the letter.

   What strikes you most as you look at the results?

5. The apostle Paul describes the truth about God as being precious and deserving preservation (2 Timothy 1:14). Yet some people treat theology more like Play-Doh—they consider themselves free to reshape it however it pleases them.

   What dangers do you see in the Play-Doh approach?

6. What are some of the "quarrel[s]," "irreverent babble," and "foolish, ignorant controversies" (2 Timothy 2:14, 16, 23) that current-day Christians get tangled up with? What effects have you seen this kind of arrogant or unkind behavior have on others?

7. What remaining questions or concerns do you have about Michael Kruger's assertion that "one can be certain and humble at the same time"?

Prayer

Ask God to open your heart to the importance of kindly yet faithfully representing his truth in our fallen world. Especially ask him to show you those areas where you most need to improve in humble orthodoxy.

Action Step

Identify people in your life who are unconcerned with biblical doctrine. For each one, try to come up with specific ways you can be a better influence in their lives when the topic of orthodoxy comes up next.

SECTION 2
With a Tear in Our Eye

How foolish prideful orthodoxy appears when we think about our sin and the salvation that Christ has provided as an act of pure grace! It's God's truth we're defending, not our own. So in our orthodoxy we're not to be promoting our own pathetic little kingdoms but magnifying God's everlasting one. Remembering our place as forgiven sinners frees us to lovingly and humbly help others know God better.

Questions

1. Take another look at the revised parable that Josh provides at the start of chapter 2. Which of the two men do you more readily identify with, and why?

   If you identify more with the theologically deep but smugly self-righteous man, what specifically do you need to repent of?

2. Josh says, "When you truly understand the doctrine of grace in the gospel, you don't go around checking people's IDs to see if they are in or out. You walk around with tears of gratefulness in your eyes, saying, 'Why in the world would he choose me?' "

Spend some time thinking about the sins God has forgiven you in Christ, the wrath you have been saved from, and the blessings you have become heir to. If you're working through this study guide with a group, name aloud at least one thing that sparks gratitude in your heart toward God.

What can you do to remember this feeling of grateful awe the next time you are tempted to condemn someone who is drifting from biblical truth?

3. Read Joshua 5:13–15, that strange but resonant story of General Joshua meeting the commander of God's army. Josh Harris says this incident shows that God "doesn't sign on to our agenda. We sign on to his."

How have you been guilty of trying to enlist God for your side rather than enlisting on his?

If you were to ask the Lord, "What do you want to

say to me right now?" how do you think he might reply?

4. Knowledge has an insidious way of puffing up our egos. So it is easy to let the correctness of our theology become more important to us than God himself is. At that point humility goes out the window and people get hurt.

Have you ever let your knowledge of theology make you arrogant? If so, describe what happened.

5. One writer described Francis Schaeffer as someone who critiqued culture "with a tear in his eye." That's humble orthodoxy. That's caring for truth while recognizing that others are sinful creatures in need of the Creator's mercy just as we are.

Think back to the most recent time you spoke up for orthodoxy with a less-than-humble attitude. How might it have been different if you'd had "a tear in your eye"?

Prayer

Thank God for his great mercies to you. Ask his help in sharing mercy with others through the good news of Jesus Christ.

Action Step

If you feel convicted about the ways in which you have been harsh toward others because of their disobedience to God's truth, apologize in a letter or e-mail or phone call. Share the story of your own forgiveness and acceptance by God.

Section 3
Repentance Starts with Me

Josh says in chapter 3, "I'll tell you what deflates my arrogance and self-righteousness faster than anything else: trying to live whatever truth I have." It's easy to criticize others for their faulty beliefs. What's harder is living out biblical doctrine ourselves. Yet that's where humble orthodoxy has to start.

Questions

1. Josh starts chapter 3 by describing his friend Justin, who manages to be gracious toward those who

criticize him on his blog, as an inspiring example of humble orthodoxy.

For you, who serves as a model for humble orthodoxy? (It could be someone you know personally or someone you've just heard or read about.) What can you learn from this person?

2. How would you describe the temperature of your desire to live out humble orthodoxy?

HOT: My heart is filled with yearning to obey God with both right doctrine and love for others.

WARM: Since starting to read this book, I've felt more and more as if humble orthodoxy is something I want in my life.

COOL: Intellectually, I guess I can see how humble orthodoxy would be a good thing. But I'm having a hard time caring much about it personally.

If the temperature of your desire is cool or warm, what's keeping it from getting hot?

3. Read the story of Josiah and the rediscovered Book of the Law in 2 Kings 22:3–20. Note especially verse 11 (Josiah's reaction when he listens to the scroll being read) and verses 18–19 (the Lord's response to Josiah).

   Josh Harris comments regarding Josiah's reaction, "This is just the kind of humility we need today. Orthodoxy shouldn't be a club to attack someone else. It should be a double-edged sword that starts by piercing our hearts, laying them bare before God so that we say, 'Forgive *us*, Lord!' "

   In our culture we don't tear our robes much. But what evidence in your life reveals that you are repentant for ways you have failed to obey God's Word?

4. The following is a report card for you. Give yourself the appropriate grades (A through F) for the

two subjects listed. Why do you give yourself these
grades?

Report card for _____	
Subject	Grade
Knowledge of biblical doctrine	
Practice of biblical doctrine	

In what particular areas of doctrine could you do a
better job of living out what you already know?

Do your limitations in living out humble orthodoxy
have to prevent you from trying to help others with
their lack of orthodoxy? Why or why not?

5. Find Numbers 20:1–13 in your Bible, and read
the full story of how Moses disobeyed God
because he was annoyed at the disobedience of
the Hebrew people. Then go to Deuteronomy
34:1–5, and read what happened as a result of
his infraction.

In discussing this event at the gushing rock, Josh says, "Here's the point: the error and sin of others never give me license to ignore the Word of God. Even when people in our culture are sinning, slandering, and tearing down truth, I have no excuse for ignoring God's commands."

Can you think of a time when you allowed the disobedience of others to draw you into disobedience? If so, describe it.

6. Josh refers to the cage stage, when people who have just discovered the importance of sound doctrine ought to be caged up because their newfound zeal can make them dangerous.

Did you go through a cage stage? If so, describe it. How has your relationship to God's truth changed since then?

What are the most important lessons about humble orthodoxy that you've learned through personal experience?

Prayer

Spend some time with God asking his forgiveness for the ways you have failed to obey his truth. Ask for his help to focus more on your own efforts to be obedient than on the ways others may be disobedient to him.

Action Step

Identify one or more practical steps you urgently need to take to practice humble orthodoxy in your life. Then do them!

SECTION 4
Living for God's Approval

What is our motive for the choices we make about what we will believe and how we will live out those beliefs? Josh says in chapter 4 that it shouldn't be to seek approval from others. It should be to seek the approval of God—the only approval that really matters. No, in this life we'll never perfectly master humble orthodoxy. And we can't expect the applause of those around us for doing it. Yet humble orthodoxy is the right thing to do. It's what God asks of us. And so to be faithful to him, we do it.

Questions

1. The reality of our world is that people tend to treat the beliefs they embrace as a kind of style to adopt, like the clothes they wear or the music they listen to. In other words, it's more about what they like and what others will think of them than it is about honoring God.

   How have you seen this belief-as-accessory approach play out? Give an example or two.

2. Compromised doctrine was rampant in Paul's day, just as it is in ours. For example, he refers to a distortion of the doctrine of the resurrection that was being debated among the church members whom Timothy served (2 Timothy 2:17–18). Read the full text of what Paul said to Timothy about this situation:

   Charge them before God not to quarrel about words, which does no good, but only ruins the hearers. Do your best to present yourself to God

as one approved, a worker who has no need to be
ashamed, rightly handling the word of truth. But
avoid irreverent babble, for it will lead people
into more and more ungodliness, and their talk
will spread like gangrene. (verses 14–17)

When it comes to the beliefs you espouse, whose
approval have you been seeking?

3. What does it mean to rightly handle the word of
truth? What does it mean to wrongly handle it?

What are the dangers of wrongly handling the word
of truth? What are the benefits of rightly handling it?

4. Josh suggests that in heaven "no one will be bragging. We all will want to talk about how wrong we
were about so many things and how kind God was
to us." He also says that in heaven "we won't be
able to stop saying, 'It was all true! It was all true!'
Every word. Every promise." In other words, humble orthodoxy will be cemented forever in heaven.

How does this vision of eternity motivate you to live out humble orthodoxy in the here and now?

5. Josh concludes the book by throwing the cold water of reality on us. He says if we are humble in the way we argue for orthodoxy, the Holy Spirit may use that to draw people to God. On the other hand, we can expect that many people will refuse right doctrine no matter how humble we are, because ultimately it's the gospel itself, not the way we represent it, that is offensive to unredeemed people. Therefore, we are to be faithful in humble orthodoxy, not for the sake of the results we hope to see, but simply because it's the right thing to do and God asks it of us.

When you have humbly spoken up for orthodoxy among people who were not orthodox, how did they react? How did you feel about their reaction?

6. What are you prepared to do differently now as a result of studying *Humble Orthodoxy*?

Prayer

Ask God to help you live now in light of eternity—with both faithfulness and a humble heart. Praise his greatness and mercy, for humble orthodoxy is ultimately all about him!

Action Step

Identify one or more fellow believers with whom you could share the message of *Humble Orthodoxy.* Choose a time to introduce this message to them so you can be part of a movement to restore loving fidelity to the gospel within the church.

Notes

1. Steve Taylor, "Whatcha Gonna Do When Your Number's Up?" *The Best We Could Find (+3 That Never Escaped),* copyright © 1988, Sparrow Records.

2. Michael J. Kruger, "Christian Humility and the World's Definition of Humility," *Canon Fodder,* March 12, 2012, www.michaeljkruger.com/christian -humility-and-the-worlds-definition-of-humility/.

3. Timothy Keller, *The Reason for God: Belief in an Age of Skepticism* (New York: Dutton, 2008), 160.

4. I've adapted a quote by Keller in which he addresses the issue of politics: "If we get our very identity, our sense of worth, from our political position, then politics is not really about politics, it is about us. Through our cause we are getting a self, our worth. That means we must despise and demonize the opposition" (Keller, *The Reason for God,* 166).

5. Greg Dutcher, *Killing Calvinism: How to Destroy a Perfectly Good Theology from the Inside* (Hudson, OH: Cruciform, 2012), 25.

6. D. A. Carson, *The Gagging of God: Christianity Confronts Pluralism* (Grand Rapids: Zondervan, 1996), 439.

7. Mark Dever, "Humble Dogmatism," Together for the Gospel, February 8, 2006, www.t4g.org/2006/02 /humble-dogmatism/.

8. Dever, "Humble Dogmatism."

9. See Justin Taylor's blog at http://thegospelcoalition .org/blogs/justintaylor/.

10. Gilbert K. Chesterton, *Orthodoxy* (1908; repr., Garden City, NY: Image, 1959), 31.

11. David Platt, *Radical: Taking Back Your Faith from the American Dream* (Colorado Springs: WaterBrook Multnomah, 2010), 142.

12. Trevin Wax, "A Critical Mind vs. a Critical Spirit," *The Gospel Coalition,* May 14, 2012, http:// thegospelcoalition.org/blogs/trevinwax/2012 /05/14/a-critical-mind-vs-a-critical-spirit/.

Acknowledgments

I'd like to thank the people who made this book possible.

First, the phrase *humble orthodoxy* was coined by my friend Eric Simmons, who pastors Redeemer Church of Arlington in Virginia. It was his encouragement for me to give a message on this topic that led to this book.

After I spoke on humble orthodoxy, John Piper strongly exhorted me to write a small book on the subject. But I didn't follow his advice exactly. Instead, I wrote a larger book called *Dug Down Deep,* with the closing chapter titled "Humble Orthodoxy." (I suppose the lesson in all this is to do what John Piper tells you the first time.)

When *Dug Down Deep* was published, many readers told me that the chapter on humble orthodoxy was their favorite and deserved to be its own book. One reader in particular asked me to make it a booklet that could be easily shared with others.

This project could only be completed because of the help and partnership of Eric Stanford, a gifted writer who was willing to take the content from my sermons and the original chapter from *Dug Down Deep* and weave and re-arrange it into a brand-new book. He also wrote the study guide. I am grateful for his excellent work and his ownership of the message.

And as with my past four books, this project was guided by my friend and editor, David Kopp. I am grateful to him and to Ken Petersen and the team at WaterBrook Mult-nomah for their enthusiasm for this message and unwavering support.

I dedicated this book to my fellow pastor Robin Boisvert. Though much older and more experienced in pastoral min-istry, he has supported me as I've learned to lead our church, has encouraged me to continue to sharpen myself theologi-cally, and has modeled running the race of faith and ministry with endurance. Thank you, Robin.

Soli Deo gloria.

About the Author

JOSHUA HARRIS is the lead pastor at Covenant Life Church in Gaithersburg, Maryland, a suburb of Washington, DC. He is also a council member of the Gospel Coalition (www.thegospelcoalition.org). This is his sixth book. He and his wife, Shannon, have three children. For information about Josh's work, online sermons, and other books, visit:

www.joshharris.com
Twitter: @HarrisJosh
Facebook: www.facebook.com/joshharris.fanpage

ERIC STANFORD is a writer and editor living in Colorado Springs, Colorado. Along with his wife, Elisa, he runs Edit Resource, LLC (www.editresource.com). They have two children.